POP & MOVIE HITS

45 Fun and Familiar Arrangements

Covering a wide variety of musical styles, the titles in this collection are proven favorites that can be enjoyed by music makers of all ages. From pop hits through the ages to epic movie music by renowned composers like Howard Shore, John Williams, Hans Zimmer, and more, the arrangements in this collection will delight players and audiences alike.

Produced by
Alfred Music Publishing Co., Inc.
P.O. Box 10003
Van Nuys, CA 91410-0003
alfred.com

Printed in USA.

ISBN-10: 0-7390-9610-9
ISBN-13: 978-0-7390-9610-9

Cover Art: Miscellaneous multimedia icons © Shutterstock / Alexander Lukin

Contents

AT LAST

Lyrics by
MACK GORDON

Music by
HARRY WARREN

AFRICA

Words and Music by
DAVID PAICH and JEFF PORCARO

Africa - 8 - 1

Africa - 8 - 3

Keyboard solo:

THE BIG BANG THEORY
Main Title

Words and Music by
ED ROBERTSON

Verse 3:

3. Aus - tra - lo - pith - e - cus would real - ly have been sick of us, de - bat - ing how we're here. They're catch - ing

23

The Big Bang Theory - 6 - 6

BRIDGE OVER TROUBLED WATER

Words and Music by
PAUL SIMON

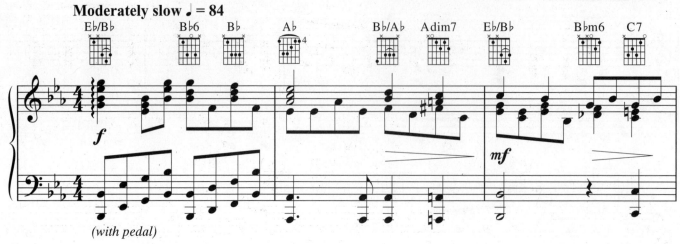

Verse 1:

1. When you're___ wea-ry,___ feel-in'___ small,

Verse 2:

CAN YOU FEEL THE LOVE TONIGHT

(from Walt Disney's *The Lion King*)

Words by
TIM RICE

Music by
ELTON JOHN

1. There's a calm surrender
2. There's a time for ev'ry-one,

to the rush of day,
if they only learn

when the heat of the roll-ing world
that the twist-ing ka-lei-do-scope

can be turned a - way.
moves us all in turn.

An en-chant-ed mo-ment,
There's a rhyme and rea - son

Can You Feel the Love Tonight - 4 - 1

CONCERNING HOBBITS

(from *The Lord of the Rings: The Fellowship of the Ring*)

By HOWARD SHORE

Moderately (♩ = 104)

Warmly (legato)

COUNT ON ME

Words and Music by
PETER HERNANDEZ, PHILIP LAWRENCE
and ARI LEVINE

Uh - huh.___ 1. If you

Verse:

ev - er find your - self stuck in the mid-dle of the sea,___ I'll sail___
toss - in' and you're turn-in', and you just___ can't___ fall a - sleep,___ I'll sing.

___ the world___ to find___ you.___ If you
___ a song___ be - side___ you.___ And if you

Count on Me - 4 - 1

DANCING QUEEN

(from *Mamma Mia!*)

Words and Music by
BENNY ANDERSSON, STIG ANDERSON
and BJÖRN ULVAEUS

Moderate disco beat ♩ = 104

Dancing Queen - 6 - 1

THE DARK KNIGHT OVERTURE

(from *The Dark Knight*)

Composed by
HANS ZIMMER
and JAMES NEWTON HOWARD

Mysteriously (♩ = 96)

The Dark Knight Overture - 13 - 1

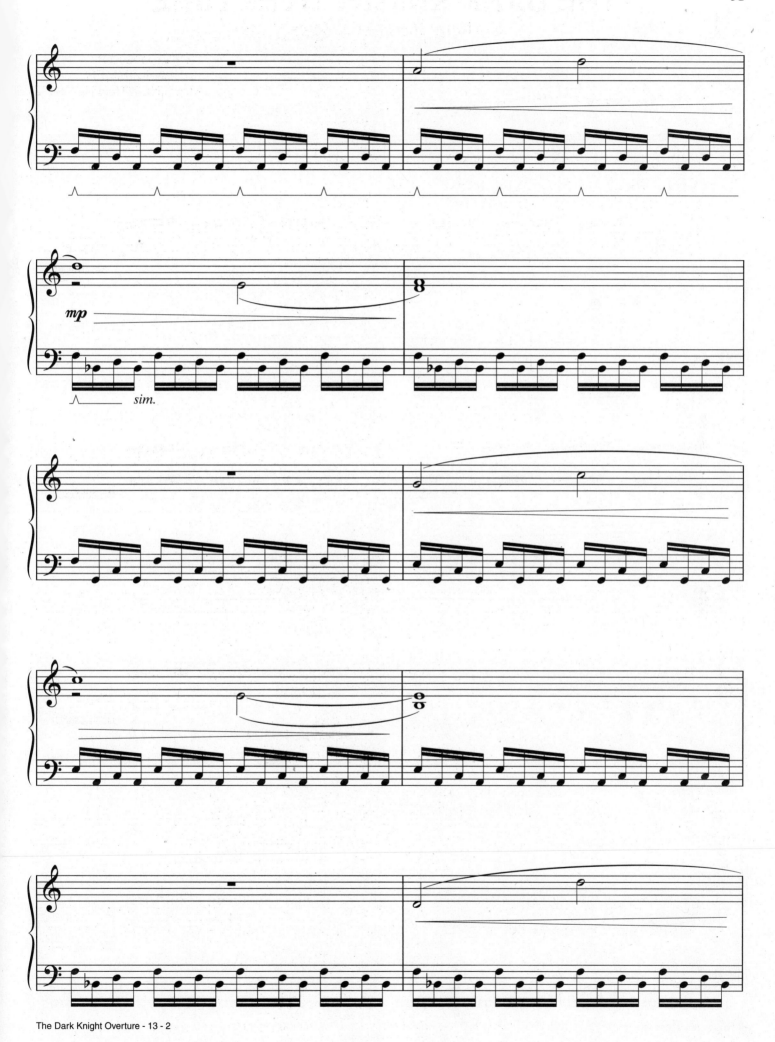

The Dark Knight Overture - 13 - 2

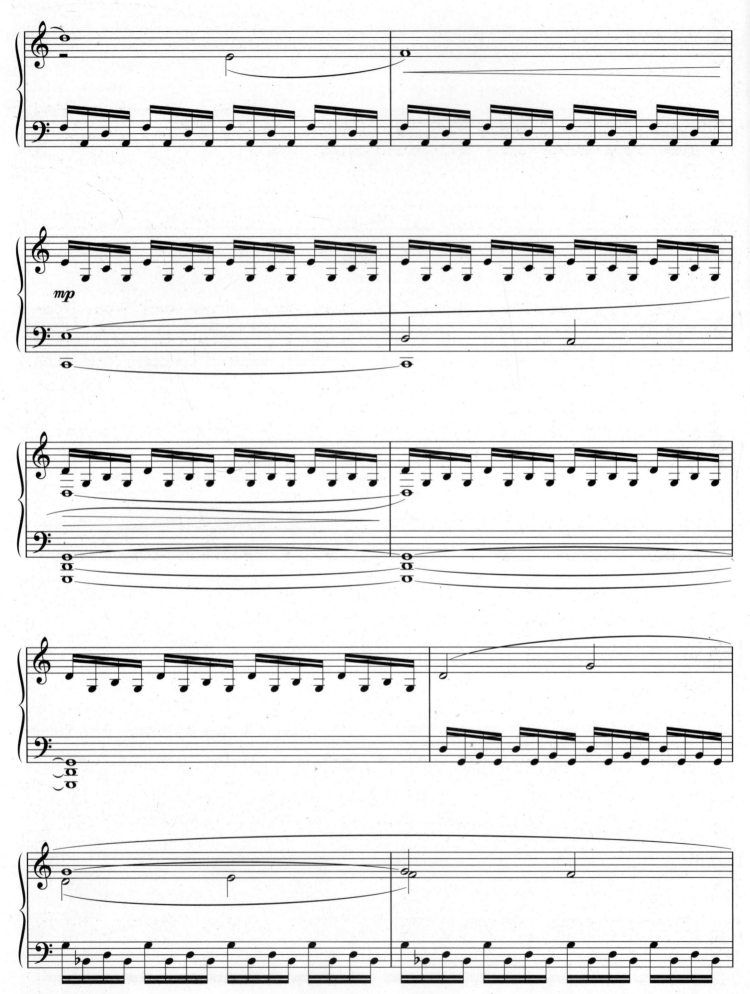

54

The Dark Knight Overture - 13 - 5

55

The Dark Knight Overture - 13 - 6

56

The Dark Knight Overture - 13 - 7

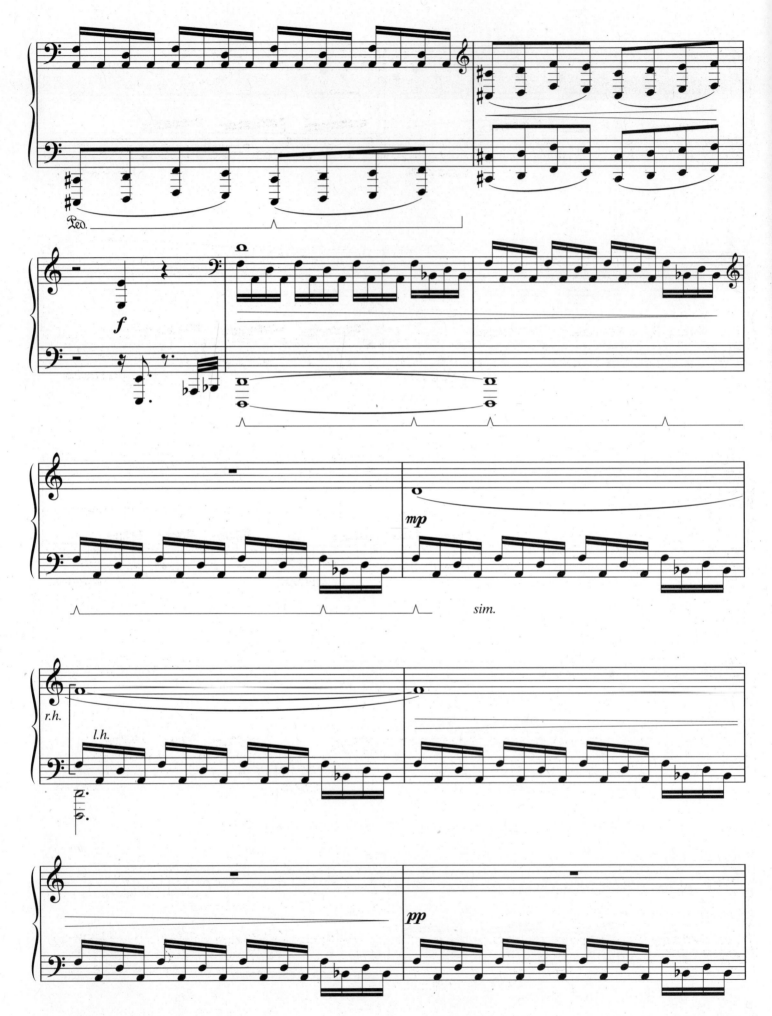

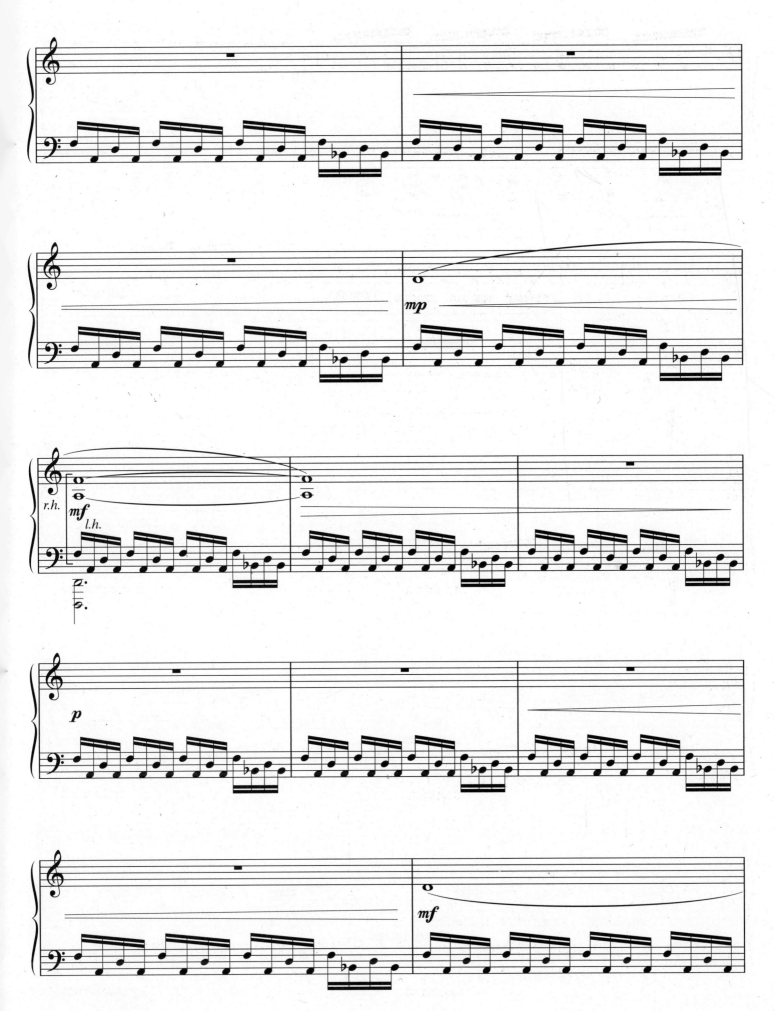

DISCOMBOBULATE

(from *Sherlock Holmes*)

Composed by
HANS ZIMMER

Discombobulate - 5 - 1

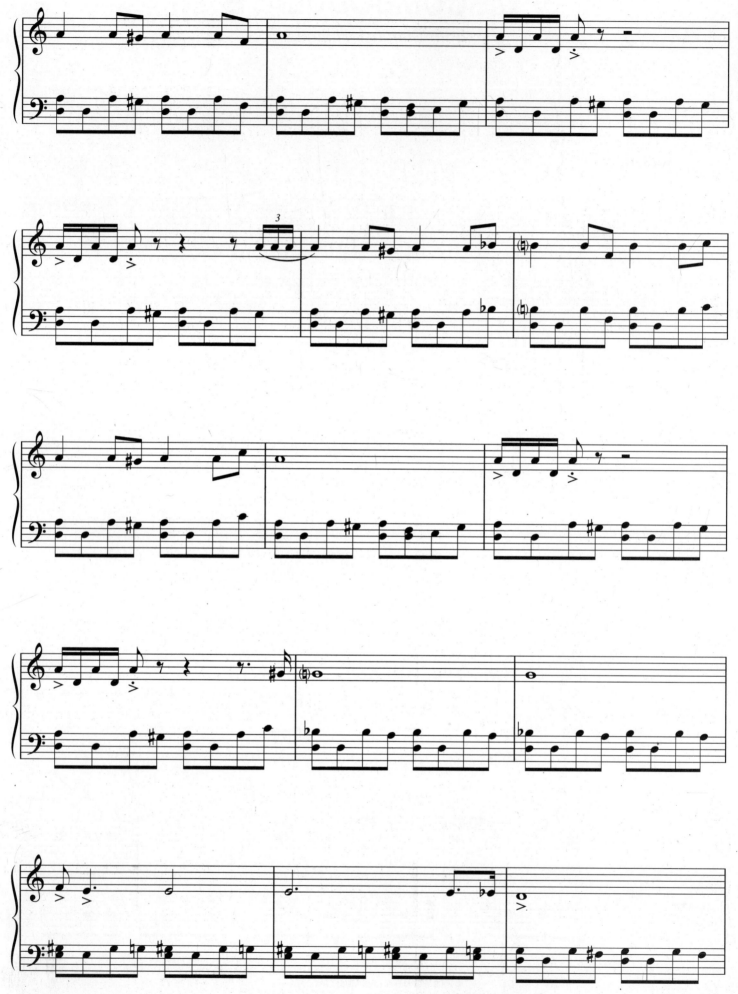

DON'T STOP BELIEVIN'

Words and Music by
JONATHAN CAIN, NEAL SCHON
and STEVE PERRY

Don't Stop Believin' - 4 - 1

69

Don't Stop Believin' - 4 - 2

70

Don't Stop Believin' - 4 - 3

EMPIRE STATE OF MIND

Words and Music by
SHAWN CARTER, ALICIA KEYS, JANET SEWELL,
ANGELA HUNTE, SYLVIA ROBINSON,
BURT KEYES and ALEXANDER SHUCKBURGH

* Original recording down 1/2 step in G♭.

Empire State of Mind - 6 - 1

Verse 1: (Sing first time only)
G
1. Grew up in a town that is famous as the place of movie scenes.
Verse 2: (Sing second time only)
2. On the avenue, there ain't never a curfew, ladies work so hard.
Cmaj7
D
G
Noise is always loud, there are sirens all around and the streets are mean.
Such a melting pot, on the corner selling rock, preachers pray to God.
Cmaj7

DYNAMITE

Words and Music by
BONNIE McKEE, TAIO CRUZ,
LUKASZ GOTTWALD, MAX MARTIN
and BENJAMIN LEVIN

Moderate dance ♩ = 116

Dynamite - 5 - 1

FALLING SLOWLY

(from *Once*)

Words and Music by
GLEN HANSARD and
MARKÉTA IRGLOVÁ

84

Moods that take me and e - rase me, and I'm paint - ed black.

Moods that take me and e - rase me, and I'm paint - ed black.

Guy:

Well, you have suf-fered e - nough and warred with your -

self. It's time that you won.

cresc.

Chorus:

too late,___ now it's gone.___

Spoken:

2, 3, 4.

mp

rit.

FORGET YOU

Words and Music by
CHRISTOPHER BROWN, PETER HERNANDEZ,
ARI LEVINE, PHILIP LAWRENCE
and THOMAS CALLAWAY

Moderately bright soul ♩ = 126

Chorus:

I see you driv-in' 'round town with the girl I love, and I'm like,

for-get you. I guess the change in my pock-et

Verse:

that falls in love with you,__ oh, oh. (Oh, sh, she's a gold - dig-ger.) Well.__

__ (Just thought you should know it.) Ooh,_____ I've

got some news for you,__ *ha ha.* { (Spoken:) *Yeah, go and run and tell your little boyfriend.* }
{ (Spoken:) *Ooh, I really hate your a** right now.* } See you

𝄋 *Chorus:*

driv - in' 'round town__ with the girl I love,__ and I'm like,__ for - get you.__

96

GIRL ON FIRE

Words and Music by
BILLY SQUIER, JEFFREY BHAKSER,
ALICIA KEYS and SALAAM REMI

Moderately, with a heavy beat ♩ = 92

Verse 1: (Sing first time only)

1. She's just a girl, and she's on fi - re.

Verse 2: (Sing second time only)

2. Looks like a girl, but she's a flame.

Hot - ter than a fan - ta - sy, lone - ly like a high - way.

So bright, she can burn your eyes, bet - ter look the oth - er way.

Girl on Fire - 7 - 1

Chorus:

102

Girl on Fire - 7 - 6

GREATEST LOVE OF ALL

Words by
LINDA CREED

Music by
MICHAEL MASSER

GONNA FLY NOW

(Theme from *Rocky*)

Words and Music by
BILL CONTI, AYN ROBBINS
and CAROL CONNORS

Moderately ♩ = 96

Gonna Fly Now - 5 - 1

110

Gonna Fly Now - 5 - 3

HARRY'S WONDROUS WORLD

(from *Harry Potter and the Sorcerer's Stone*)

Composed by
JOHN WILLIAMS

Harry's Wondrous World - 11 - 1

114

Victoriously

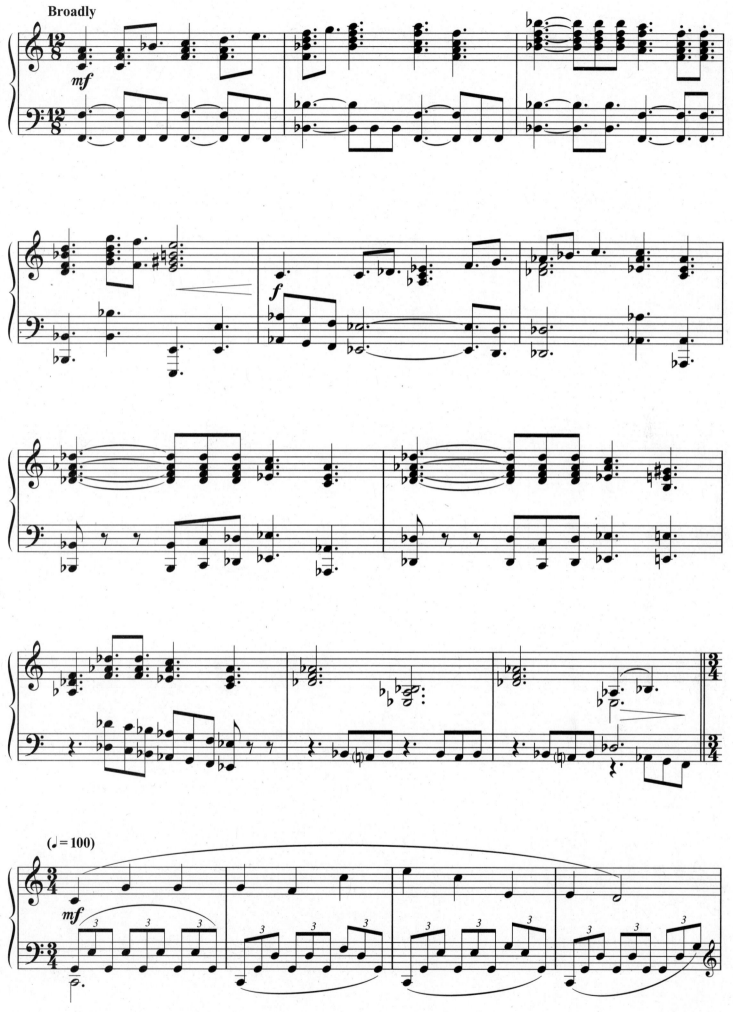

122

HEDWIG'S THEME

(from *Harry Potter and the Sorcerer's Stone*)

Composed by
JOHN WILLIAMS

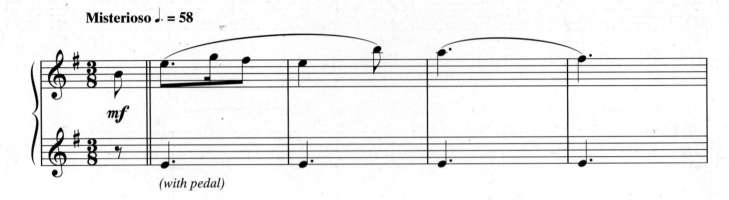

(with pedal)

126

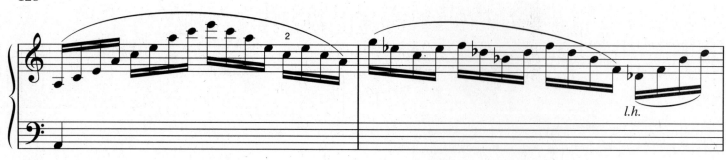

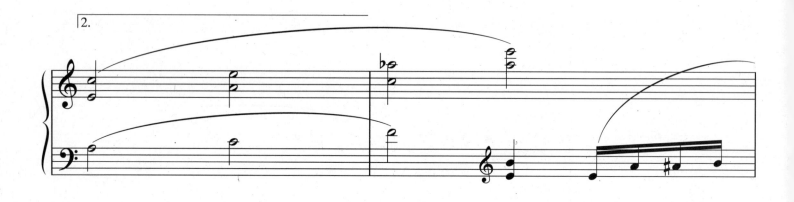

I DON'T WANT TO MISS A THING

(from *Armageddon*)

Words and Music by
DIANE WARREN

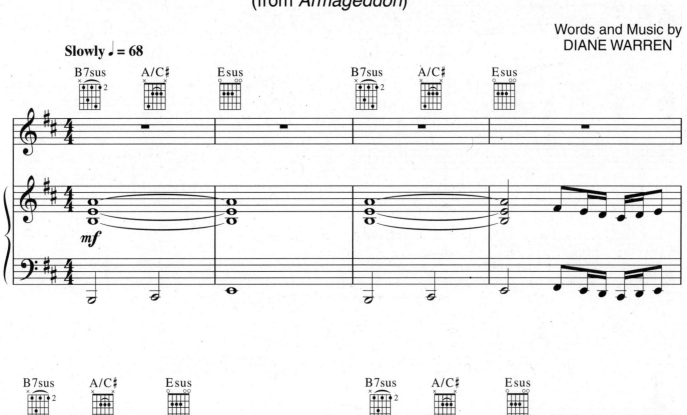

1. I could

Verse 1:

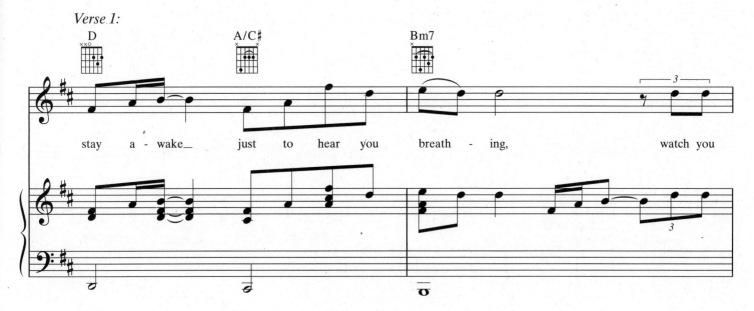

stay a - wake___ just to hear you breath - ing, watch you

I Don't Want to Miss a Thing - 7 - 1

Chorus:

I SAW HER STANDING THERE

Words and Music by
JOHN LENNON and PAUL McCARTNEY

1. Well, she was just

Verses 1 & 2:

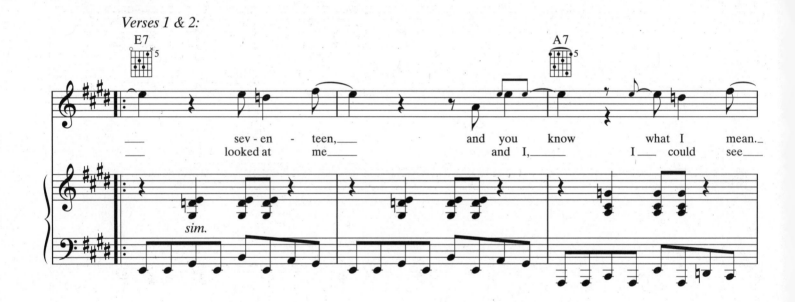

sev - en - teen,___ and you know what I mean.
looked at me___ and I,___ I __ could see___

And the way she looked was way be-yond com-pare.
that be-fore too long I __ fell in love_ with her.

And be - fore too long, I____ fell in love__ with her.__

Now, I'll nev - er dance__

with an - oth - er, ooh,____ { when I } { since I }

saw her stand - ing there.__

To Coda ⊕

Guitar solo:

THEME FROM "ICE CASTLES"
(Through the Eyes of Love)

Lyrics by
CAROLE BAYER SAGER

Music by
MARVIN HAMLISCH

Slowly, with expression ♩ = 69

Lyrics:
1. Please, don't let this feel-ing end. It's ev-'ry-thing I am, ev-'ry-thing I
(2.) now I can take the time. I can see my life as it comes up
3. Please, don't let this feel-ing end. It might not come a-gain, and I want to re-

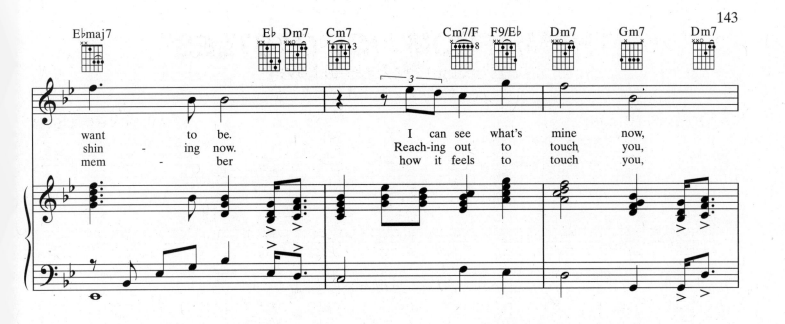

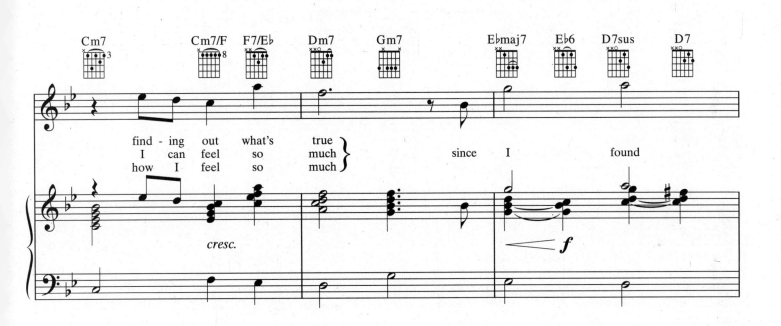

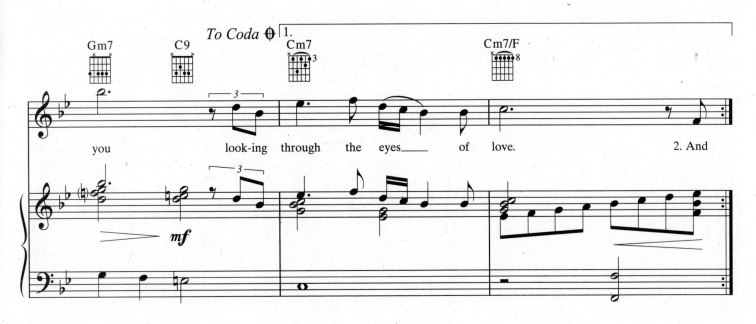

INTO THE WEST

(from *The Lord Of The Rings: The Return Of The King*)

Words and Music by
HOWARD SHORE, FRAN WALSH
and ANNIE LENNOX

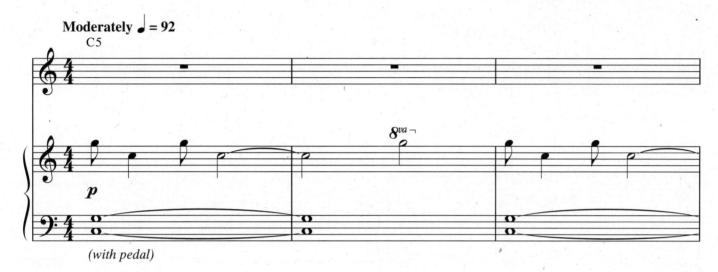

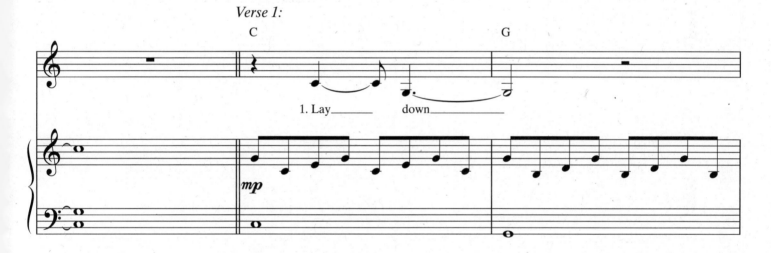

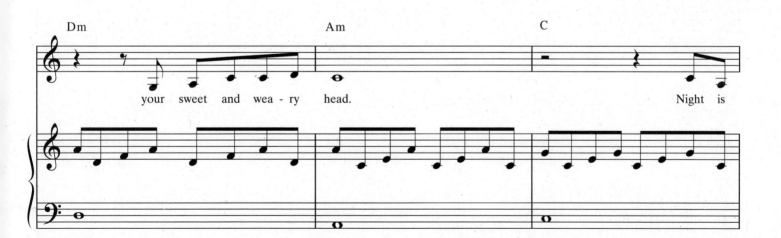

Into the West - 7 - 1

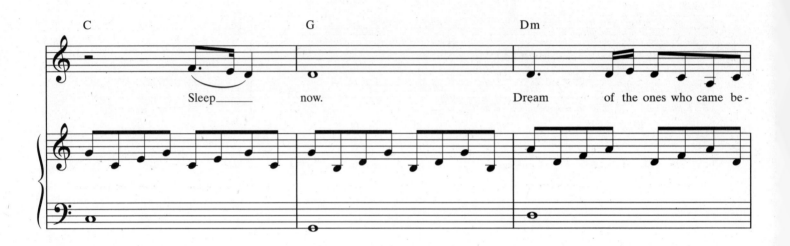

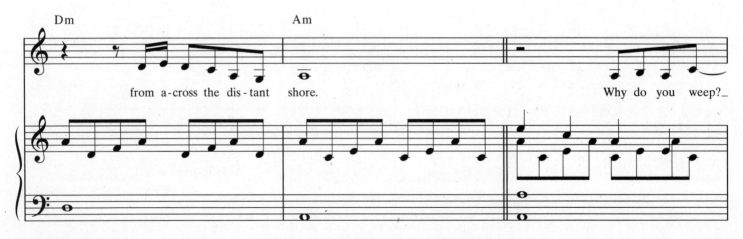

in - to the world of night

through shad-ows fall - ing   out of mem-o-ry and

time.   Don't say

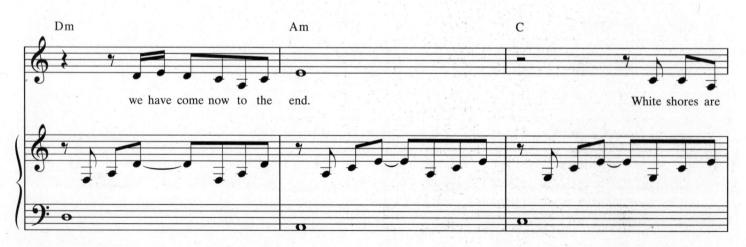

we have come now to the end.   White shores are

IF I DIE YOUNG

Words and Music by
KIMBERLY PERRY

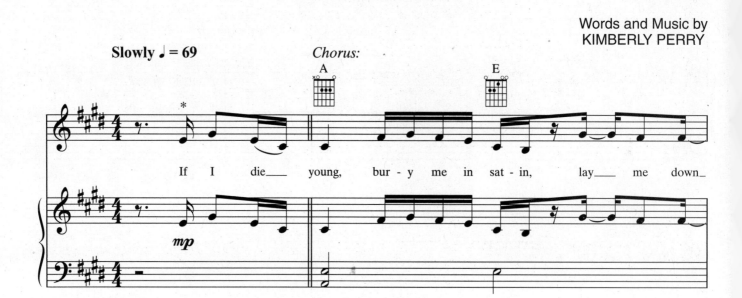

*All vocals written at pitch.

If I Die Young - 8 - 1

Verse 1:

KISS FROM A ROSE

Words and Music by
SEAL

165

166

LILY'S THEME
(Main Theme from *Harry Potter and the Deathly Hallows Part 2*)

Composed by ALEXANDRE DESPLAT

Slowly (♩ = 72)

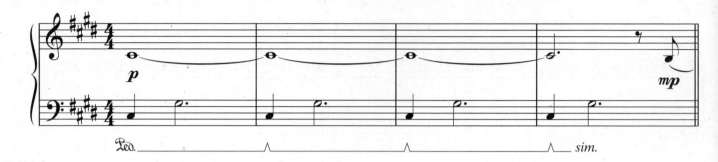

Lily's Theme - 2 - 1

Lily's Theme - 2 - 2

THEME FROM "*LOVE AFFAIR*"
(a.k.a. "Piano Solo")

By ENNIO MORRICONE

Gently, flowing

(with pedal)

MAKE YOU FEEL MY LOVE

Words and Music by
BOB DYLAN

THE JAMES BOND THEME

(from *Dr. No*)

By MONTY NORMAN

The James Bond Theme - 3 - 1

With a slight swing feel

THE NOTEBOOK
(Main Title)

Written by
AARON ZIGMAN

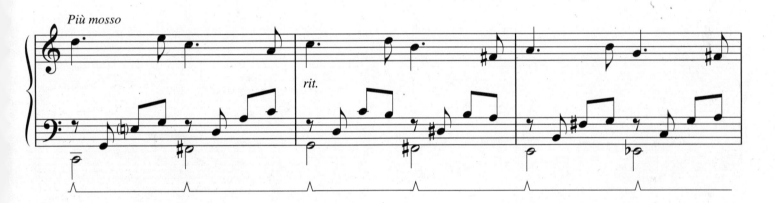

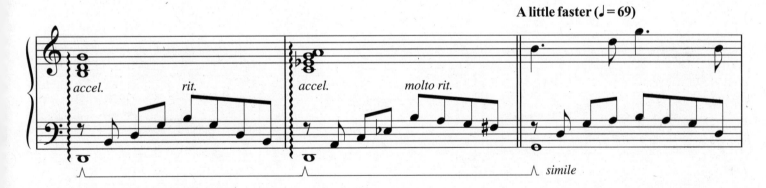

The Notebook - 3 - 1

180

OUT HERE ON MY OWN
(from *Fame*)

Lyrics by
LESLEY GORE

Music by
MICHAEL GORE

OVER THE RAINBOW

(from *The Wizard of Oz*)

Lyrics by
E.Y. HARBURG

Music by
HAROLD ARLEN

Over the Rainbow - 3 - 1

186

Over the Rainbow - 3 - 2

Over the Rainbow - 3 - 3

THE PINK PANTHER

(from *The Pink Panther*)

Composed by HENRY MANCINI

Verse:

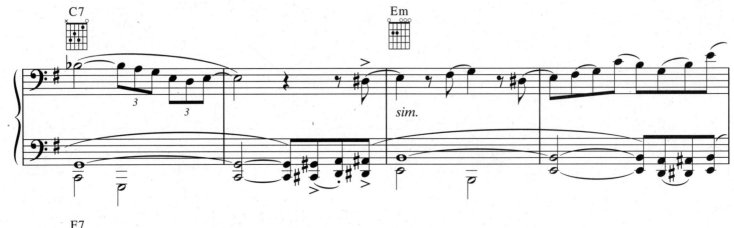

The Pink Panther - 4 - 1

Bridge:
Swing

The Pink Panther - 4 - 4

THE PRAYER

Italian Lyric by
ALBERTO TESTA and TONY RENIS

Words and Music by
CAROLE BAYER SAGER and DAVID FOSTER

Slowly, with expression (♩ = 72)

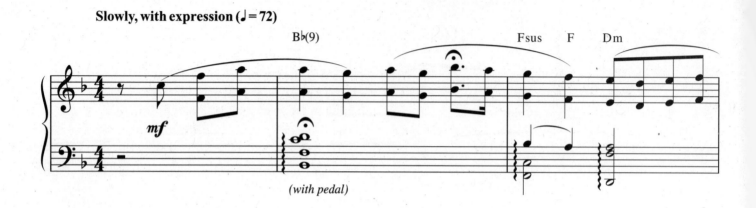

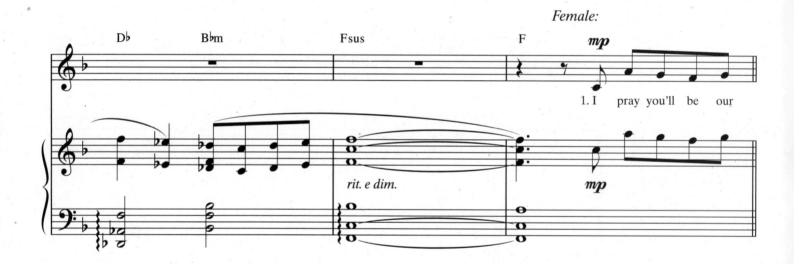

Verse 1:

The Prayer - 8 - 1

194

The Prayer - 8 - 3

198

The Prayer - 8 - 7

STAIRWAY TO HEAVEN

Words and Music by
JIMMY PAGE and ROBERT PLANT

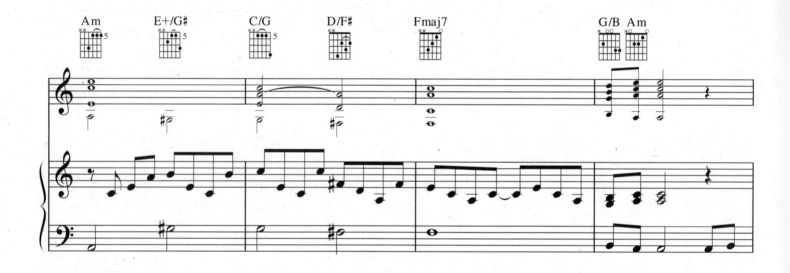

Stairway to Heaven - 12 - 1

206

211

Stairway to Heaven - 12 - 12

SONG OF THE LONELY MOUNTAIN

Lyrics by
NEIL FINN

Music Composed by
NEIL FINN, DAVID DONALDSON,
DAVID LONG, STEVE ROCHE
and JANET RODDICK

Song of the Lonely Mountain - 9 - 1

216

long - for - got - ten gold. We lay____ un - der the Mis - ty____ Moun - tains_ cold, in slum - bers deep_____ and dreams_ of gold. We must a - wake,____ our lives_____ to make,_____ and in the dark-

217

Song of the Lonely Mountain - 9 - 6

TIME

(from *Inception*)

By
HANS ZIMMER

Slowly (♩ = 60)

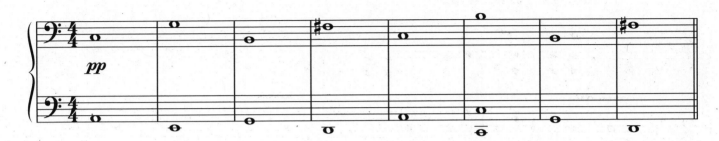

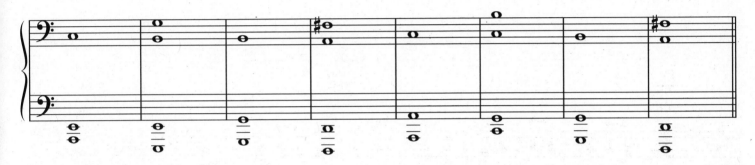

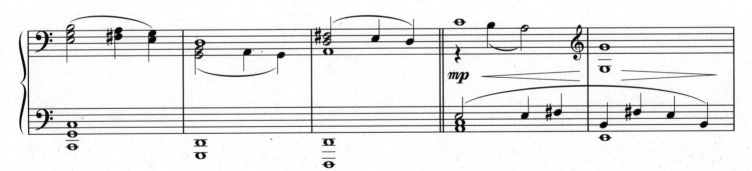

Time - 3 - 1

TEARDROPS ON MY GUITAR

Words and Music by
TAYLOR SWIFT and LIZ ROSE

226

Teardrops on My Guitar - 6 - 3

A VERY RESPECTABLE HOBBIT

(from *The Hobbit: An Unexpected Journey*)

Music by
HOWARD SHORE

A Very Respectable Hobbit - 2 - 1

VICTOR'S PIANO SOLO

(from *Corpse Bride*)

Composed by
DANNY ELFMAN

Victor's Piano Solo - 2 - 1

(cluster chords)

*F𝄪 = G♮

WHEN I WAS YOUR MAN

Words and Music by
PHILIP LAWRENCE, ANDREW WYATT,
BRUNO MARS and ARI LEVINE

Chorus:

238

When I Was Your Man - 5 - 5

YOU LIGHT UP MY LIFE

Words and Music by
JOE BROOKS

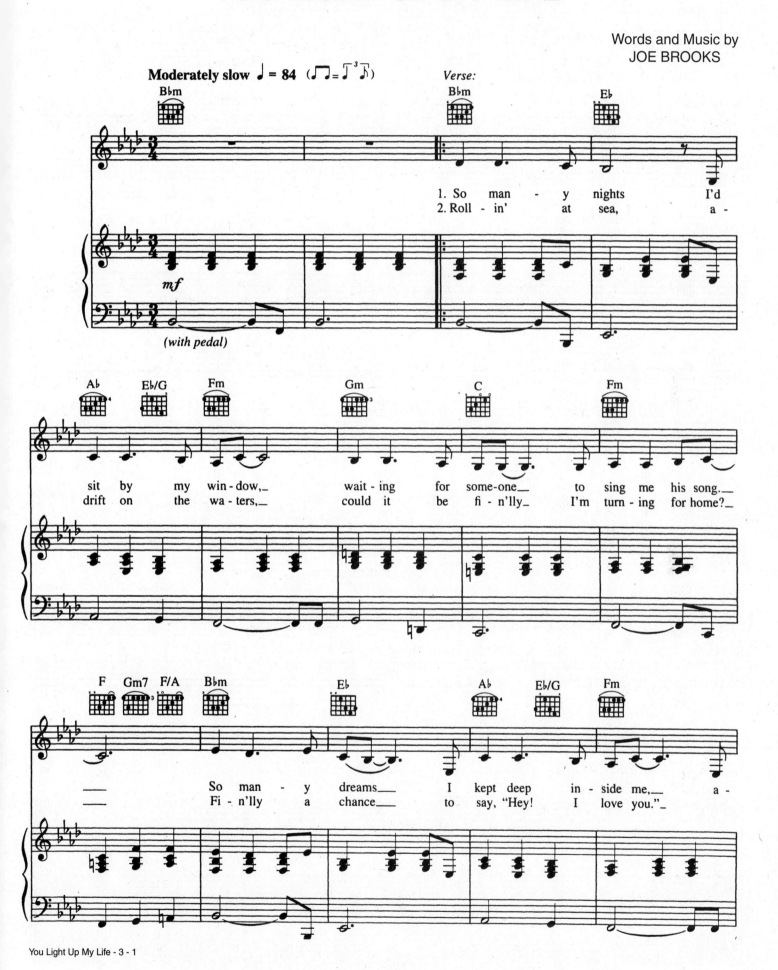

You Light Up My Life - 3 - 1

240

ZIP-A-DEE-DOO-DAH

(from Walt Disney's "Song of the South")

Words by
RAY GILBERT

Music by
ALLIE WRUBEL

Lyrics:
Zip - a - dee - doo - dah, zip - a - dee - ay,____ my, oh my,____ what a won - der - ful day!____

Plen - ty of sun - shine head - in' my way,____ zip - a - dee - doo - dah, zip - a - dee - ay.____ Mis - ter

Zip-A-Dee-Doo-Dah - 2 - 1

YOU RAISE ME UP

Words and Music by
ROLF LOVLAND and
BRENDAN GRAHAM

Slowly ♩ = 60

You Raise Me Up - 5 - 1